I WAS THE JUKEBOX

THE BARNARD WOMEN
POETS PRIZE

Edited by Saskia Hamilton

2003 *Figment* RebeccaWolff
Chosen by Eavan Boland and Claudia Rankine

2004 *The Return Message* Tessa Rumsey
Chosen by Jorie Graham

2005 *Orient Point* Julie Sheehan
Chosen by Linda Gregg

2006 *Dance Dance Revolution* Cathy Park Hong
Chosen by Adrienne Rich

2007 *Woman Reading to the Sea* Lisa Williams
Chosen by Joyce Carol Oates

2009 *I Was the Jukebox* Sandra Beasley
Chosen by Joy Harjo

Every image is a sign of the future and the past, stamped fiercely into the present. Every statement we utter by thought or voice makes a path through time and space. Those shaped in poetry can be especially potent. In Sandra Beasley's *I Was the Jukebox*, there is no wavering of image or sign. These poems are fresh, crisp, and muscular. They are decisive and fearless. Every object, icon, or historical moment has a soul with a voice. In these poems these soulful ones elbow their way to the surface of the page, smartly into the contemporary now.

I WAS THE JUKEBOX

Poems

Sandra Beasley

~~Sandra Beasley~~

With deepest gratitude to the U.S. Embassy for these days in Cyprus and these inspiring conversations.

Aera!
Onwards!

Cheers, SB
November 9, 2017

W. W. NORTON & COMPANY
New York   London

For information about permission to reproduce selections from this book,
write to Permissions, W. W. Norton & Company, Inc.,
500 Fifth Avenue, New York, NY 10110

For information about special discounts for bulk purchases,
please contact W. W. Norton Special Sales at
specialsales@wwnorton.com or 800-233-4830

Manufacturing by Courier Westford
Book design by JAM design
Production manager: Andrew Marasia

Library of Congress Cataloging-in-Publication Data

Beasley, Sandra.
I was the jukebox : poems / Sandra Beasley.—1st ed.
p. cm.
ISBN 978-0-393-07651-6 (hardcover)
I. Title.
PS3602.E2558I25 2010
811'.6—dc22
                                    2009040996

ISBN 978-0-393-33966-6 pbk.

W. W. Norton & Company, Inc.
500 Fifth Avenue, New York, N.Y. 10110
www.wwnorton.com

W. W. Norton & Company Ltd.
Castle House, 75/76 Wells Street, London W1T 3QT

2 3 4 5 6 7 8 9 0

For Christina,
who has her own stories to tell

CONTENTS

The Sand Speaks / 17

Orchis Speaks / 18

Another Failed Poem about the Greeks / 20

The Minotaur Speaks / 22

Cast of Thousands / 24

The World War Speaks / 26

Antietam / 27

Making History / 28

Love Poem for College / 30

My God / 31

You Were You / 32

Returning to the Land of 1,000 Dances / 33

I Don't Fear Death / 35

Immortality / 37

To the Lions / 39

*　*　*

The Hotel Devotion / 43

Signs / 45

Signs / 46

Signs / 47

The Piano Speaks / 48

The Eggplant Speaks / 49

The Plays of Lilliput / 51

Another Failed Poem about Music / 52

Japanese Water Bomb / 54

Making the Crane / 56

The Cutting Board / 57

Love Poem for Oxidation / 59

Osiris Speaks / 60

The Story / 62

The Translator / 63

*   *   *

Exits / 67

Plenty / 68

The Natives Are Restless / 70

The Parade / 72

Beauty / 73

In the Deep / 75

Love Poem for Wednesday / 76

Fugue / 78

Vocation / 79

Another Failed Poem about Starlings / 80

Unit of Measure / 82

The Platypus Speaks / 84

Love Poem for Los Angeles / 86

Antiquity / 88

Proposal / 90

ACKNOWLEDGMENTS

My thanks to journals in which earlier versions of these poems appeared:

32 Poems: "You Were You" and "Vocation"

AGNI Online: "I Don't Fear Death," "My God," and "Love Poem for Wednesday"

Barn Owl Review: "Proposal"

Barrelhouse: "Antiquity"

The Believer: "Cast of Thousands"

Black Warrior Review: "Returning to the Land of 1,000 Dances," "The Eggplant Speaks," and "The Platypus Speaks" (as part of the chapbook *Bitch and Brew: Sestinas*)

Blackbird: "Making History," "The Minotaur Speaks," and "The Parade"

Blue Fifth Review: "Love Poem for Los Angeles," "Love Poem for College," and "Signs" ["Before he would leave he'd empty his pockets"]

Cave Wall: "The Sand Speaks," "Another Failed Poem about the Greeks," and "To the Lions"

Delaware Poetry Review: "The Plays of Lilliput"

DIAGRAM: "Making the Crane"

Drunken Boat: "Orchis Speaks" (as "Orchis") and "Fugue"

Florida Review: "The Story"

Gulf Coast: "Antietam" and "Another Failed Poem about Music" (as "Solo")

Hayden's Ferry Review: "Beauty" and "In the Deep"

Hotel Amerika: "Immortality" and "The Translator"

Linebreak: "The Natives Are Restless" and "The Hotel Devotion"

The Normal School: "Japanese Water Bomb," "Love Poem for Oxidation," and "Plenty"

Potomac Review: "The Cutting Board"

Pleiades: "Osiris Speaks" and "Exits"

Poetry: "The Piano Speaks" and "Unit of Measure"

Reed Magazine: "Signs" (as "After Miscarriage") ["Each morning her husband rides his mower across the lawn"]

The Scrambler: "Signs" (as "The Orchard") ["The day before his appointment they went"]

Slate: "The World War Speaks"

"Signs" (as "After Miscarriage") also appeared in 2005 *Best New Poets*, coedited by George Garrett and Jeb Livingood. "Another Failed Poem about Starlings" appeared in a Big Game Books chapbook to celebrate a 2007 d. a. levy lives series reading, as well as Pittsburgh IsReads. "Cast of Thousands" appeared in the Narrow House *i. e. Reader*. "Proposal," "The Sand Speaks," and "The Platypus Speaks" appeared on *Verse Daily*.

Many of these poems came out of NaPoWriMo, shepherded by Maureen Thorson. My thanks to her and the many writers who have inspired me, conspired with me, and helped along the way, including Erika Meitner, Carly Sachs, Aimee Nezhukumatathil, Bruce Covey, Josh Bell, Hailey Leithauser, John Surowiecki, Rhett Iseman Trull, Deborah Ager, Jehanne Dubrow, Lauren Cardwell, Natalie E. Illum, Monica Jacobe, and Holly Jones.

Thank you, Joy Harjo and the forces behind the Barnard Women Poets Prize: Saskia Hamilton, Jill Bialosky, Adrienne Davich, Alison Liss, and everyone at W. W. Norton.

While working on this book I received support from the Sewanee Writers' Conference (including a valuable manuscript review from Mary Jo Salter), the Jentel Artist Residency Program, and *Poets & Writers* (through the 2008 Maureen Egen Writers Exchange Award). I've welcomed the camaraderie of those at American University, the University of Virginia, New Issues Poetry & Prose, the Writer's Center, the Arts Club of Washington, and the *American Scholar*. Particular gratitude goes to Rita Dove, Gregory Orr, Lisa Russ Spaar, Richard McCann, Myra Sklarew, and Mary Lynn Kotz for their mentorship and kindness.

A huge thank-you to my family—for the trips made, toasts offered, copies stockpiled, and the myriad ways you have shown your love and encouragement.

Finally, to Adam, who keeps me going on this wild ride.

*   *   *

THE SAND SPEAKS

I'm fluid and omnivorous, the casual
kiss. I'll knock up your oysters.
I'll eat your diamonds. I'm a mutt, no
one thing at all, just the size that counts

and if you're animal small enough, come;
if you're vegetable small enough, come;
if you're mineral small enough, come.
Mothers, brush me from the hands

of your children. Lovers, shake me
from the cuffs of your pants. Draw
a line, make it my mouth: I'll name
your country. I'm a Yes-man at heart.

Let's play Hide and Go Drown. Let's play
Pearls for His Eyes. When the men fall
I like the way their arms touch, their legs
touch. There are always more men, men

who bring bags big enough to hold
each other. A man who kneels down
with a smaller bag, cups and pours, cups
and pours, as if I could prove anything.

ORCHIS SPEAKS

Imagine having one good leg and keeping
your ovary in it. I grow tired. I grow
fickle. I grow on corpses.
I am secretly excited when trees catch fire.
My mother lives in New Guinea and weighs a ton.
In the cloud forests of Costa Rica my smallest sisters
mutter *Bite me* through purple lips seen only
with a magnifying glass. In the 1800s,
scientists claimed we could not be grown in a lab;
so we did, just to spite them. Now
every year brings some humiliating study
on the aunt who reeks of carrion, or the uncle
in the Yunnan who won't stop fertilizing himself.
I won't be another table pet.
Sometimes at the Farmers' Market
a woman with yapping dogs looks at me
and all I can do is droop. *God, no.*
I dream sometimes of Greece, two legs,
the festival where I drank too much wine.
When the priestess said *Come here* I came.
When she said *Stop* I kept coming. The guests
made a red circle around me. They grabbed my hair,
my arm, chanting, my other arm, pulling,

clawing the skin until it surrendered from muscle,
the unbearable tearing, and I wake—
unable to scream with this lush, exploded tongue.

ANOTHER FAILED POEM
ABOUT THE GREEKS

His sword dripped blood. His helmet gleamed.
He dragged a Gorgon's head behind him.

As first dates go, this was problematic.
He itched and fidgeted. He said *Could I*

save something for you? But I was all out
of maidens bound to rocks. So I took him

on a roller coaster, wedging in next to
his breastplated body in the little car.

He put his arm around me, as the Greeks do.
On the first dip he laughed. On the first drop

he clutched my shoulder and screamed like
a catamite. When we ratcheted to a full stop

he said *Again.* We went on the Scrambler,
the Apple Turnover, the Log Flume.

We went on the Pirate Ship three times,
swooshing forward, back, upside down,

· · ·

and he cried *Aera!* waving his sword,
until the operator asked him to please keep

all swords inside the car. He was a good sport,
letting the drachmas fall out of his pockets;

sparing the girl who spilled punch on his shield;
waving as I rode the carousel's hippogriff

though it was a slow ride, and I made him
hold my purse. On the way home

he said *We should do this again sometime,*
though we both knew it would never happen

since he was Greek, of course, and dead,
and somewhere a maiden rattled in her chains.

THE MINOTAUR SPEAKS

The queen lay in the hollow
of a wooden cow so my father
would mount her, his white hide
glistening like a raw moon.
To love is to look up, up, up.
She named me Asterius,
the starry one. When the king
heard my birth cry, he raised
black curtains to every window
in Crete. He began to build.
My father was led away by a rope
around his neck. My mother
gave me the apple of her breast,
and I bit it off. To love is to feed
and feed again. My room
has thirty-two walls, no doors,
no chair, no light, no mirror.
I touch a face that is leather
and horns and mine, mine, mine.
They say this man has flaxen hair,
a mouth so fine the gods
beg him to speak. They say
my death will make him
a hero. Everyone loves a hero,

but a hero only loves you
until he reaches the next island.
This is my only island. To love
is to unwind the long thread
of your heart and, at the end, tie
a noose. Love, come and get me.

CAST OF THOUSANDS

When they make a movie of this war
I am minute ninety-seven, soot tears
applied with a Q-tip, the one whose roof
collapses on her head before
her pie is done. Look how I look at you—
the apple and the apple's knife still rolled
into my skirt, eyes wide as gin. The blast,
then ash. The director cried *Cut!*
More ash, he said, and they bombed me again.
My death is the clip they send to the Academy;
later they will kill me in Spanish, then French.
I will die on mute, on airplanes, row after row
of my tiny, touchscreened dying. My love,
I have joined the cast of thousands: me
and the plucky urchin, the scared infantryman,
me and the woman whose laminated beauty
sells gyros on every Greek storefront—
a useful anyone who advances the story,
then drops away. In your dream
six months from now I'll make my cameo
as the customer with an unfocused smile,
offering a twenty as the register
begins to shake and smolder under your hands.
The coins will rise and spit silver into the air.

The coins will rise and spit silver into the air.
They buried my village a house at a time,
unable to sort a body holding from a body held,
and in minute ninety-six you can see me raise
my arms as if to keep the sky from falling.

THE WORLD WAR SPEAKS

When I was born, two incisors
had already come through the gum.
They gave me a silver bell to chew on,
brought me home in a wicker basket,
and kept me by the stove's coal heat.
Every morning my mother boiled
a huge vat of mustard greens,
steam drifting over to my crib and
after a few hours, souring into a gas.
I breathed it all in. I began to walk
so they fitted me with braces.
I began to run, so they fitted me
with books: Mars, hydrogen, Mongolia.
I learned to dig a deeper kind of ditch.
I learned to start a fire in three minutes.
I learned to sharpen a pencil into
a bayonet. Sometimes at night
I'd sneak into the house of our neighbors,
into the hall outside their bedroom,
and watch as they moved over each
other like slow, moonlit fish.
Sometimes my mother would comb
my father's hair with her fingertips,
but that was it. They wanted an only
child: the child to end all children.

ANTIETAM

We all went in a yellow school bus,
on a Tuesday. We sang the whole way up.
We tried to picture the bodies stacked three deep
on either side of that zigzag fence.
We tried to picture 23,000 of anything.
It wasn't that pretty. The dirt smelled like cats.
Nobody knew who the statues were. Where was
Stonewall Jackson? We wanted Stonewall on his horse.
The old cannons were puny. We asked about fireworks.
Our guide said that sometimes, the land still let go
of fragments from the war—a gold button, a bullet,
a tooth migrating to the surface. We searched around.
On the way back to the bus a boy tripped me and I fell—
skidding hard along the ground, gravel lodging
in the skin of my palms. I cried the whole way home.
After a week, the rocks were gone.
My mother said our bodies can digest anything,
but that's a lie. Sometimes, at night, I feel
the battlefield moving inside of me.

MAKING HISTORY

All I know of the Spanish-American War
is what Virginia boys, kept safe at college,
etched into the mortar with their pencils
so that leaning against a brick wall
a hundred years later, I can make out
Cuba Libre! and *Remember the* Maine*!*
I don't remember the *Maine*, only
that a Cuba Libre is made of rum, Coke,
and lime. What I know of sacrifice is

the tin spoons that always fall into
my dorm room radiator. Cereal: spoon.
Ice milk: spoon. The world is lousy
with spoons. The world is lousy
with lentils, flash bombs, lo-fi, hi-speed.
Somewhere is a petition I should be
signing. Somewhere a parakeet is
driving a tractor, and I am missing it.
A pair of scissors is thrown and the boy

catches it with his arm, the blade sinking
inches deep, so fast there is no blood.
His roommate says *What do we do now?*
Pull it out, says the boy, but no one wants

to be the one to pull it out. That's when
they turn the camera off. Some nights
I dream we meet: *You have to help me,*
he says. *Cuba is burning.* I reach into his arm.
I pull out spoon after spoon after spoon.

LOVE POEM FOR COLLEGE

You hit on me. You hit on everyone.
You pour gallons of lightning punch
into a trash bag, promising that sobriety
is just a 2 A.M. Waffle House away.
You are always under construction.
The earth shall be inherited by your trucks.
Every semester brings new commandments.
Your blackboards are suspiciously green.
You pop your collar. You roll your skirt.
You tell me you don't care, then you
sneak off to the stall on the third floor
and throw up. You hit me, once.
You hit everyone, once. You
streak the Chancellor's house.
You steal beakers from Chem class.
When you say you are sorry,
you mean you've left your heart out
on the train tracks again. Later
we will all wonder if you were
the best of us, but you were probably
just the most frantic. We swarmed
like fireflies in our jar before someone
lifted the lid off. We pierced the sky
with our panting, involuntary light.

MY GOD

My god is a short god. My god wears jeans.
When he swims, he has a lazy breaststroke.
When he gardens, he uses his bare hands.
My god watches reruns of late night talk shows.
My god could levitate but prefers the stairs
and if available, the fireman's pole. My god
loves bacon. My god's afraid of sharks.
My god thinks the only way to define a country
is with water. My god thinks eventually,
we will come around on ear candling. My god
spits chaw. My god never flosses.
My god reads Proust. My god never
graduated. He smiles when astronauts reach
zero gravity and say *My god, My god.*
My god is knitting one very big sweater.
My god is teaching his terrier to beg.
My god didn't mean for icebergs. My god
didn't mean for machetes. Sometimes
a sparrow lands in the hands of my god
and he cups it, gently. It never wants to leave
and so, it never notices that even if it tried
my god has too good a grip, my god, my god.

YOU WERE YOU

I dreamt we were in your favorite bar:
You were you, I was the jukebox.
I played Sam Cooke for you,
but you didn't look over once.
I wanted to dance. I wanted a scotch.
I wanted you to take your hand off of her.
You were wearing your best smile
and the shirt that makes your eyes green.
If you had asked, I'd have told you
her hair looked like plastic.
But then, my mouth was plastic.
I weighed 300 pounds.
I glittered like 1972.
A man tried to seduce me with quarters
but I could hear his truck outside,
still running. I was loyal to you.
I played Aretha, Marvin, the Reverend Al.
You kissed her all the way out the door.
Later, I tried to make my own music,
humming one circuit against the other,
running the needle up and down.
The bubbles in my blood were singing.
In the morning, they came to repair me.

RETURNING TO THE LAND OF
1,000 DANCES

It's brutal how I've missed your shout and twist,
your Sallies Mustang, Sallies tall and long.
Your Checker chubby, your Locomotion,
your Potato mashed and Pony broken.
Dear country, how I have longed to get down
and dirty. I'm no Fred, you're no Ginger.

Your boots weren't made for waltzing gingerly,
and we don't garnish rotgut with a twist.
How I've missed our country ways. Let's go down
to Harvey's Moon, where I've been gone so long
some jerk bumped my score from the now-broken
pinball game. I've always loved the motion

perpetual, the whiplash emotion
of finger on flipper, the fizz ginger
makes with gin, bottle spun till it's broken.
One kiss, my dear country, and please don't twist
away. Inside the bunker all along
it was you I dreamed of—hunkering down

as shit pooled at our feet, as shells rained down,
my trigger finger the only motion—
it was you. While the other grunts had long

debates over Mary Ann or Ginger
I reached for the dip of your back, the twist
of your hip, and a beat never broken.

Don't wait until hallowed ground needs breaking
to call me up. I've laid my shovel down
anyway, giving the dirt one last twist.
I came home for an earthier motion
and my dear, I don't mean farming ginger.
Every life is a thousand dances long

and the horizontal ones all belong
to you. Before the record sounds broken:
Move with me. A house of bread and ginger
awaits us but before we settle down,
before it's all going through the motions,
put on a skirt, put your hair in a twist,

wear a parachute. It's a long way down—
The Yo-Yo, broken. The Jerk in motion.
We Ginger and Chicken, we turn and twist.

I DON'T FEAR DEATH

But what I'm really picturing
is Omaha: field after field

of sorghum crisp to my touch
and one house on a high hill,

sheets on the line. You tell me
everything ceases, that even

our fingernails give up, but
what I really believe is that

we keep growing: infinite corn,
husk yielding to green husk.

I look back on the miles
connecting me to Earth, think

I'd have never worn those shoes.
I slip them off like anything

borrowed. The clouds are thin
and yellow, smelling of

. . .

fireworks and salt. In Omaha,
the town votes me Queen of

Everything. You are the slow
dance, the last ring of smoke:

to be held tight, and then only
this colder air between us.

IMMORTALITY

Face it: I will never
appear on the flipside of a nickel,
or as a balloon floating down Fifth Avenue;
no one will give my name to a variety of rosebush,
or a way to throw fastballs, or a beetle
with four strange, silvery wings.

They say my spit's helixes will swim in the children
of my children but that's nothing more
than a simple whip graft, the way
a pear tree is bullied into fruit. My heart
is one yellow marble waiting in a swarm of yellow marbles,
waiting for someone to chalk lines of play, waiting

for the thumb of God. Inertia
is a poor man's immortality. Even
the ancient recipes have failed us now—
no more gilded eyelids or canopic jars, no more
baklava baking in the crypt
of my jaw. Call me

selfish, but who doesn't dream
of being both kite and wind, boat and ocean?
I want to be the ball and the bat and the mound

and the sweat and the grass.
I want to be the vampire who drinks
a tall cool glass of me so he can live forever.

TO THE LIONS

Stop perhapsing—
the savannah will not save you.

Everything is dead or dying;
running, or about to run.

Time to stop lifting the wallet
from the corpse's pocket.

Time to gather your most
fuckable queens.

Isn't that the sun, draped
around your neck?

Stop this kitty kitty nonsense,
this apologetic yawning:

Show us why your tongue
is covered in hooks.

*   *   *

THE HOTEL DEVOTION

In the Hotel Devotion
there is no running water,

no power, no stairs,
no bed. There is only

the woman who holds
a river in her mouth,

fireflies in her hands,
the woman who bends

for you, opens for you.
There is only this book,

this pen in your hand,
your name the only name.

Outside, pigeons bellying
down the alleys of night.

Inside, this sadness
blooming in your throat.

Sometimes a handful of
light is mistaken for love. I

did not know it was a river
until I tried to swallow.

SIGNS

The day before his appointment they went
to the orchard. They always went in June,

and driving up they listened to Patsy Cline
because they always listened to Patsy Cline.

He stayed in the trees until she said *Come down*
and on the last rung this new thing—her hand

pressed against his back, as if he were a child
who needed catching. He hated her. And

she lifted the basket of cherries to show him
their pale skins, hemorrhaged with sweetness.

SIGNS

Each morning her husband rides his mower across the lawn,
then back again. Each night he runs his hand aground
on the helpless bank of her belly.

She knows they expect needles, knives, firehot brands.
They need her to own the cinders, a hole
that can burn itself clean away.

How, then, to explain that for weeks her baby had been
a trout, a nesting of cool bones and pale flesh
sewn to the bottom of a muddy river?

She compliments the peach cobbler. She feels.
She does. And she has always known her fingers to be a net
she could not lace tight enough.

SIGNS

Before he would leave he'd empty his pockets
onto the dresser and she'd seen it, that last night,

every coin landing face down. *Don't go*, she'd said.
And he'd laughed like he always did at her signs:

crows on the lawn, a hang-up call, salt on the floor.
He'd left before dawn, wanting her to sleep in.

She should have known as soon as she broke eggs
for an omelet and the pink embryos came sliding out;

she should have cleared out her freezer, knowing
the casseroles would come. With all her signs,

why did she put on the cheap bra that morning?
She remembers the chaplain at her door,

holding his hat like an apology. How he'd
placed his hands on her shoulders and she'd said

God. Under his hands, her flesh welling past
nylon straps: that dumb beast in harness, that hope.

THE PIANO SPEAKS

after Erik Satie

For an hour I forgot my fat self,
my neurotic innards, my addiction to alignment.

For an hour I forgot my fear of rain.

For an hour I was a salamander
shimmying through the kelp in search of shore,
and under his fingers the notes slid loose
from my belly in a long jellyrope of eggs
that took root in the mud. And what

would hatch, I did not know—
a lie. A waltz. An apostle of glass.

For an hour I stood on two legs
and ran. For an hour I panted and galloped.

For an hour I was a maple tree,
and under the summer of his fingers
the notes seeded and winged away

in the clutch of small, elegant helicopters.

THE EGGPLANT SPEAKS

The bartender always studies my face.
It's his job. He wipes counters, cuts limes, lines
up the bottles. I want him to like me.
I say, *An eggplant walks into a bar.*
Wait, no. An eggplant would waddle. Then lean,
because she has no arms. What was the joke?

I'm now realizing I forget the joke.
The bartender asks, *Why the purple face?*
Oh Bartender. This is why women lean
and tip 40 percent. It's a thin line
between love and bribery in a bar.
I've swallowed scorpions, I could say. *Save me*

from my own bitterness. But that's just me
and a ninth-century Bedouin joke
that might, just might, work in a Baghdad bar.
A ninth-century one. Sometimes I face
a life alone as my own best punch line.
Scotch, like salt, draws out the bitter. I lean

because, Bartender, the universe leans:
this constellation of seeds inside me
expands at all hours along unknown lines

maybe magnetic, or some quantum joke.
My face distances itself from my face.
This is something you often see in bars,

an effect unfairly blamed on the bar
itself. Look at your body, long and lean
in a white button-down, your stubbled face.
I'm sorry. It's cosmic nightshade in me,
taking root, strangling what should be a joke.
Oh Bartender. They'll say that you mainlined,

that the infection coursed your arms' bloodlines.
A foolish woman walks into a bar
and says *Take my arms, please.* Half of a joke.
You say *How many eggplants*—here, you lean—
to roof a house?   *Beats the hell out of me,*
she says. It's your job to study her face,

to stock the pick-up lines, to make her lean.
Eggplant, bar: *Depends how thin you slice me.*
I'm tired of jokes, she says, hiding her face.

THE PLAYS OF LILLIPUT

They are gathering the curtains
of my hair. They are priming
the fog machine in my lap.
O brass band of my heart!
O concession stand of my knee!
O audience, shuffling to your
seats, your shoes tickling
my thigh. Tonight, the actors
tune their voices. They put on
habits. They bead up rosaries.
Who doesn't dream of clapping
the living daylights out of
such small, obedient faces?
O dressing room shoulder!
O sound booth shoulder!
O audience. Who doesn't dream
of the spotlight burst into flame,
and all of you running into
the safety of my open mouth?

ANOTHER FAILED POEM ABOUT MUSIC

I love the small tyranny of it,
the musician standing with his arm raised
through measure upon measure,
waiting for a moment to strike his wand—

the ding that pierces a twelve-part din.
Technical name: *struck idiophone.*

In his first concerto Franz Liszt
gave an entire solo to the triangle,
notes pit-
pattering like acid rain.

I can tell you when to use steel,
when to use glass. Wooden spoon,
knitting needle, chicken bone:
I'm an expert at striking.

Even the name, *triangle,* is a perfect
betrayal—sides two and three will never
come together. The music is born

in the gap. Music is born in barns,
in bars, in apartments newly empty.
Listen: It's a line with legs.

Listen: It's a struck idiot.
Listen: It's my fortune, the cookie
who sings *Lovers in triangle*
not on square.

JAPANESE WATER BOMB

How she reaches to eat off the man's plate just
as he says *So I've been meaning to say this*—
How she swerves the fork back to her own bowl,

the way a woman who fails to hail a taxi will act
as if she meant to tuck some hair behind her ear.
How he's doing this in a cheap tea house.

How he tells her *I don't know how to do this.*
End this? How she is wary. *No*, he says, *how
to make space inside this thing without destroying it.*

How a Japanese water bomb is thirty-two useless
folds of paper until the maker gives it breath.
How the difference between an igloo and a block

of ice is only the body sheltered beneath it.
How she parses scallions from the pile of salmon
before declaring *Tea-cured*? *It's fucking raw.*

How she leans her head to his shoulder. How he
wants to flinch and doesn't. How the moment splits,
a mitosis of love and chronology: how he is

•   •   •

her present. How she has become his past.

How a man can't go about selling a bridge, even if a bridge is the one good thing he has to sell.

MAKING THE CRANE

Preparation is the art of leaving lines in:
before you can make that crane you must
invert the valley, low right to high left.
Then you must base the bird, pulling
inside out, outside to middle, and up.
Flip. Repeat. Crease those legs.
Reverse the fold. Define her neck,
define her tail, run the bone knife flat.
Dip each wing down and pull them
apart, flattening her back. If she means
to stay by your dinner plate, press your
mouth to that belly and push the air in.
If she means to fly, grip her head and tail,
pull so she flaps in the sky of your palm.
If she's good luck, thread a sharp needle
and hang her with her thousand sisters.
When she laughs it is only a crab scuttling
the length of that gullet. When she cries
it is only the weeping of rice against stone.

THE CUTTING BOARD

waits, clean. It's only
a common Tuesday.
Your heart eases open,
peony past bloom.
The aorta splits. You

die on a kitchen floor,
pots dryboiling.
In yellow permissions
of sleep I am granted
a curtained hour

to pack the picnic basket
of your belly: bread, oil,
cooling lamb, pour of wine,
wild rice, peppers
red and sweet. Then

nothing. Mouth slack,
acids ungurgled.
Hands and sheet
I must fold back above
the body. I wake from years

•   •   •

of your counting out
almonds for the car,
sandwiches for the plane,
and now this one journey
for which I cannot feed you.

LOVE POEM FOR OXIDATION

You are ascendant valence; you are
reactant loss. You are da Vinci's aerial screw
lifting up and up, the puny genius
waving from inside like an oblivious

god. The spoon, tarnished.
The tarnation of apple. Antsy Juliet
and the balcony breaking beneath you.
Love, let me count the waves as they wash

over the sump wall, iron loosening to rust,
flaking away. You are the sunburn
where there is no sun, a canary nested
in the rib cage of a miner. *All clear*, sings

his skeleton. *All mine*, sings the canary.
Romeo, if you think I am losing it,
of course I am losing it. This is all about
the losing of it, blood ache, a slow

striptease of protein. You are the simplest
mathematics, rounding off to the nearest
dying. *Be mine*, says the skeleton, flashing
a smile that could seduce flesh from bone.

OSIRIS SPEAKS

I left my heart in San Francisco.
I left my viscera in the Netherlands.
I left my liver on the 42 Line, headed
from Farragut Square to the White House.
I left my occipital lobe in Reno.
I left my corneas in Tangier.
I left one foot in a courthouse,
and one in a traveling circus. I had hoped
to find you, Isis, before the fish swam
between my legs and swallowed,
but now I navigate the Seine,
sharing a scaled belly with the ashes
of Joan of Arc. So I left my pride in Paris.
I left a vertebra in Venice. On Murano,
my clavicle became the mouth of a bowl.
I left my mouth on Mount Everest,
holding every apology I had meant to offer
and while they chattered in sad fury,
I sowed my teeth in an arctic field.
Now there is little left of me: Fingers
with nothing to tickle. Hands with nothing
to grasp. The small bones of my ears
do their xylophone dance while the small

cusps of my wrist bones pretend to be
ears. Every king, in the end, is his only
audience. Every queen picks up the pieces.
Isis, every fish in that river is a child
of mine. You are my net. Hold me.

THE STORY

As soon as you put two things
together, you have a story.
                    —John Baldessari

In the story I am the nightingale, and you
are usually the hotplate; though occasionally

you are the subway token, and I am the Queen
of Norway. Once I was copper ore, running

in thin sheets through the gut of a mountain,
and you were the favorite rooster, pecking corn

from the hand of the farmer's wife. Sometimes
the story struggles to hold it all: the runaway

train and the cheetah. The booster rocket and
the handgun. Now I am strung on a rosary.

Now you are ripening on a tree. Years pass,
as if the story has forgotten us. Then a priest

holds the paper to a candle flame; and the nun's
love letters, writ in lemon juice, come to life.

THE TRANSLATOR

He paid me to carry his words
in my mouth—
to give him the cut of sky,
the color of beef.
To give him *please.*
To give him *thank you.*
To give him tea kettle, spider, tango.
I ate at his table.
I moved into his basement.
I made a dictionary of sighs—
when to order takeout,
when to play Stravinsky, when
to tell the woman to take her clothes
and go. Soon he was dying.
I can't breathe, he said, so I said
I can't breathe. My heart, he said,
so I said *My heart.* It was my wrist
the nurse held, my chest
under the stethoscope. *I'm sorry*,
said the doctor, and my throat
became a coffin
they could not open.

*   *   *

EXITS

In the end, a man bolts from the ice-cream parlor.
In the end, a woman gets in the convertible.
In the end, a hat check girl slaps her gangster.
In the end, a gambler kisses his bookie.
In the end, there will often be a helpful sign:

The End, and the iris of the camera tightening shut.
Someone will turn on the lights. Someone will pick up
the popcorn. Except this time the room stays dark.
There is no light switch on your side of the door.
And it's your passport, your suitcase, your young wife;

the Chief of Police saying *We'll process your papers*;
his gunman saying *Your papers have been processed.*
You realize there's been a terrible mistake,
that this is not the light comedy you signed up for.
Someone nailed the trapdoor shut. Somewhere

your parachute is waiting. All over America
good mothers are baking pie after pie after pie.
Good mothers, drinking glass after glass after glass.
This only works if you play the part as written.
In the gingerbread house, something must burn.

PLENTY

The goats were swollen with wheat,
bass overflowing the banks. Too many
potatoes. Monstrous zucchini. The sheep,
hustling across Wyoming shoulder to shoulder,
became a great blanket fevering the Midwest.
News crews from Florida showed children
paddling helplessly among the oranges,
looking for a place to stand.
We called to the scientists but
they were busy watching as petri dishes
grew into petri pools, petri lakes.
They had no cure for the multiplicative.
We called the firemen but they were
up in trees, tossing down cat after cat.
We called to Jesus and He came
in a set of a thousand, robed and sandaled;
every city got a Jesus and ours stood
on the street corner like Santa Claus,
waving His tin bell. *You have been
blessed by plenty*, He told us. We begged
for less. We wanted one slice left
in the pan, one measure left in the song.
We wanted the ramen, the penny jar, coupons

cut and saved. *Impoverish us*, we prayed,
our voices forming a faithful din
so great that no one could decipher it.

THE NATIVES ARE RESTLESS

Of course you invited them in: faces painted
like trick-or-treaters, carrying pointy spears.
The youngest clutched his goat, the tallest
her stack of bowls, and you had rooms to spare.
They fill the house with song and drums;
they show you the dance for morning, the dance
for evening, the dance for mowing the lawn.
They yank the dustcovers off your heart.
Now you have sheets to iron, skirts to mend.
You wish your husband was here to see this.
You are useful. You are adored. They want
marrow for breakfast, pancakes for supper.
They like to watch you work the griddle.
You try to teach the youngest to play checkers,
but he wants to play Tied to the Stake, Capture
the Blonde. Some nights they get a little loud
in their chanting, and you worry where the cats
disappeared to. But then they show some
unexpected kindness: a vertebrae necklace,
a cool compress, a broth of leeks and onion.
They need your gentle hand, your quick stitch.
They need for you to live, at least until they need
to kill you. Some nights the house rises up

on chicken legs and turns in circles around you.
You are their egg—their center, the warmth
and flutter. They will wait as long as they can.

THE PARADE

The parade will feature red dragons,
drums, sixty horses,
and a sharpshooter in kimono.

Children will receive small flags to wave.
Women will receive small children to clutch.
You may note we offer five varieties
of yellow ribbon.
You may note we've drained the gunpowder
from your firecrackers.

Look at how the cherry blossoms
squawk and circle
before sinking their pink talons
into the monuments.
The monuments play dead.
They are fleshy with granite.

Think of these barricades as an embrace
of concrete. Look—
how your country longs to hold you.

BEAUTY

That night, something howled outside.
I opened the door. It was Beauty. Beauty
was muddy and senseless. I let her in.
I tried to towel her off, and she bit me.
She drank water from a plastic bowl,
then crawled under the table and fell asleep.
The next day Beauty ate eggs, a little raw beef.
For hours I worked the burrs from her hair,
so matted I had to shave it in the end.
She licked at the bare skin. We decided
to keep her. She learned a few tricks.
When Beauty played dead, clocks shivered.
Beauty built a Sistine Chapel of chicken bones.
Beauty could tune her whining like a violin.
Sometimes she let the kids ride her around
the living room. And when she left a mess
we rubbed her nose in it, so she'd understand
that even Beauty makes mistakes. We loved her.
She liked to gather flowers in her mouth.
We bought Beauty a red coat, a steel collar.
We liked to think she had chosen us.
Then one day Beauty ran off, as strays do.
I told the kids it would have been cruel

to keep her all to ourselves. They don't
believe me. My daughter refuses to eat,
dreams of Beauty beading on her skin like rain.
My son models Play-Doh in the Classical style:
He has taken away our arms and our heads.

IN THE DEEP

The boys are fifteen
and fuckwild:

Fuck the glass fish,
they say, bodies pulsing
with injected neon;
fuck the nautilus, nursing
its bubble of salted air.

What they love is
this crumple of muscle
suctioned to the tank's
darkest corner—
Fuck her blue rings.
Fuck her three hearts.

The octopus cradles
a baby doll, the doll's head
stuffed with krill. *Fuck
yeah,* they say, watching

as she pokes one eye
out, then the other.

LOVE POEM FOR WEDNESDAY

You're the day after Tuesday, before eternity.
You're the day we ran out of tomatoes
and used tiny packets of ketchup instead.

You are salt, no salt, too much salt, a hangover.
You hold the breath of an abandoned cave.
Sometimes you surprise me with your

aurora borealis and I'll pull over to watch you;
I'll wait in the dark shivering fields of you.
But mostly, not. My friends don't care for you

or your lessons from the life of a minor god.
Can you hit the high C in our anthem?
Can you bench press a national disaster?

I fear for you, Wednesday. Your papers
are never in order. Your boots track in mud.
You're the day I realized I didn't even like him,

and the day I still said *Yes, yes, yes.*
Sometimes I think you and I should elope,
and leave this house of cards to shuffle itself.

· · ·

You are love, no love, too much love, a cuckold.
You are the loneliest of the three bears, hoping
to come home and find someone in your bed.

FUGUE

The trees cup light in their low branches.
The sidewalks are dying.
I am walking from pharmacy to pharmacy.
I pull bits of teeth from my mouth.
I pull concrete from my mouth.
Ahead, another green cross is winking.
The song in my mouth is dying.
The name in my mouth is not my name.
The trees cup pharmacies in their branches.
I offer the sidewalk a tourniquet.
I pull the knot from my mouth.
I tighten the truth with my hands.
The trees thank me for stopping.
A green cross turns away, embarrassed.
Here, let me hold that blood for you:
I need something to do with my hands.
Here, will you hold this name for me?
I need something to do with my mouth.

VOCATION

For six months I dealt Baccarat in a casino.
For six months I played Brahms in a mall.
For six months I arranged museum dioramas;
my hands were too small for the Paleolithic
and when they reassigned me to lichens, I quit.
I type ninety-one words per minute, all of them
Help. Yes, I speak Dewey Decimal.
I speak Russian, Latin, a smattering of Tlingit.
I can balance seven dinner plates on my arm.
All I want to do is sit on a veranda while
a hard rain falls around me. I'll file your 1099s.
I'll make love to strangers of your choice.
I'll do whatever you want, as long as I can do it
on that veranda. If it calls you, it's your calling,
right? Once I asked a broker what he loved
about his job, and he said *Making a killing.*
Once I asked a serial killer what made him
get up in the morning, and he said *The people.*

ANOTHER FAILED POEM ABOUT STARLINGS

I'll have a starling shall be taught to speak
Nothing but "Mortimer," and give it to him
To keep his anger still in motion.
                              —Henry IV, Part 1, act 1, scene 3

You need to know they have no call
of their own, only what they are given.
You need to know Eugene Schieffelin

was rich, and dreamed of bringing
the birds of Shakespeare to America,

and as he stood in Central Park releasing
handfuls of starlings, *Sturnus vulgaris*,
we applauded as they settled in the eaves
of the museum. Now,

100 years and 200 million starlings later,
their fat mimicry crowds every nest—

they rise in flocks of 10,000,
devour cherries by the metric ton,
wrestle small planes to the ground.
You need to know we've tried everything:

.   .   .

plastic owls, Cobalt-60, our government's
best recipe for starling pie. In Illinois

a man is teaching starlings to speak,
wiring his farm with the murmur
of *Schieffelin, Schieffelin, Schieffelin,*

so that we might know the monster by the name
of his Frankenstein. You need to know

how light they were, lifting from his hands,

their bodies shimmering with hunger.

UNIT OF MEASURE

All can be measured by the standard of the capybara.
Everyone is lesser than or greater than the capybara.
Everything is taller or shorter than the capybara.
Everything is mistaken for a Brazilian dance craze
more or less frequently than the capybara.
Everyone eats greater or fewer watermelons
than the capybara. Everyone eats more or less bark.
Everyone barks more than or less than the capybara,
who also whistles, clicks, grunts, and emits what is known
as his *alarm squeal*. Everyone is more or less alarmed
than a capybara, who—because his back legs
are longer than his front legs—feels like
he is going downhill at all times.
Everyone is more or less a *master of grasses*
than the capybara. Or going by the scientific name,
more or less *Hydrochoerus hydrochaeris*—
or, going by the Greek translation, more or less
water hog. Everyone is more or less
of a fish than the capybara, defined as the outermost realm
of fishdom by the sixteenth-century Catholic Church.
Everyone is eaten more or less often for Lent than
the capybara. Shredded, spiced, and served over plantains,
everything tastes more or less like pork
than the capybara. Before you decide that you are

greater than or lesser than a capybara, consider
that while the Brazilian capybara breeds only once a year,
the Venezuelan variety mates continuously.
Consider the last time you mated continuously.
Consider the year of your childhood when you had
exactly as many teeth as the capybara—
twenty—and all yours fell out, and all his
kept growing. Consider how his skin stretches
in only one direction. Accept that you are stretchier
than the capybara. Accept that you have foolishly
distributed your eyes, ears, and nostrils
all over your face. Accept that now you will never be able
to sleep underwater. Accept that the fish
will never gather to your capybara body offering
their soft, finned love. *One of us*, they say, *one of us*,
but they will not say it to you.

THE PLATYPUS SPEAKS

As far as the *duck-billed platypus* goes,
I'd like to point out there's no other kind
of platypus. You don't say *horse-hooved deer*
or *moth-winged butterfly*. A beast should be
her own best description. I deserve that,
having survived a hundred thousand years

of *You would make a fine-looking hat.* Years
take their toll: the right ovary that goes
on the fritz every time, flat feet, and that
tangled mess of sex—ten different kinds
of X, Y, and yeah, blind dates tend to be
a disaster. We're no sluts like the deer,

though; June through October only, my dear.
Then we build deeper burrows for the year,
each dirt plug a form of daycare. *To be
a mom must suck*, or so the saying goes,
except we've got no teats. Only a kind
of belly-gulley, where milk pools so that

the platypups can lap it up. Take that,
Disney. Bambi's mom was never a deer
daiquiri. Takes a particular kind

of woman to do that for seven years,
twins every time, while the deadbeat dad goes
back to his bachelor pad. He must be

so satisfied—lazy as a queen bee—
stroking his only weapons, hind spurs that
barnacled to his ankles. Out he goes
with enough venom to kill angry deer,
but would he save me from hunters? No. Years
teach me not to expect a card, a kind

Mother's Day word, or flowers of any kind.
There's no alimony in the wild, beware.
Even minor developments take years.
But evolution's crawl has its perks: that
way I track electric waves, swift as deer,
swiveling to go as the hot shrimp goes,

each soul-spark a kind of beacon. If that
makes me the bad guy, Disney, be a dear
and live all my years. You'll see how it goes.

LOVE POEM FOR LOS ANGELES

Two hundred years ago, we set out west one
oath at a time, a long game of Telephone: You

are our strangest echo, the promise of Great American
Self-Storage. Los Angeles, I love your red-and-white

strip joints, your car dealerships, your Bob Hope Hall
of Patriotism. I love the graze of your fingernails,

your slow sparklers of palm trees, your buildings silver
and inscrutable, this constant haze as if a battle just

ended and your bloodied asking *Did we win? Did we win?*
Los Angeles, take off your sunglasses, roll your window

down; I like it when you let your hair whip into knots.
Los Angeles, even your salads glisten with fish and

though I know you dream of living forever, cancer
looks good on you. Los Angeles, I love the ways

·   ·   ·

you misunderstand me: *Jew* for *blue*, *erosion* for *ocean*.
I am rushing your Russians, I am cold for your gold.

When I tell you I'm married, all you say is *I do.*
When I say *Don't get hurt* you hear *Flirt harder.*

ANTIQUITY

We are living in someone's antiquity.
They will study our compromises—
how we used two faucets for one sink,
how we wired and cemented our teeth,
how our kids spent hours stacking pennies
in cardboard tubes. They'll wonder
why we ever took ourselves so seriously,
measuring each ideal serving of meat
with a deck of playing cards, declaring
"Estelle" the official state soil of Alaska,
going door to door every ten years to ask:
Do you live alone? With an indoor toilet?
In antiquity it will always be past bedtime.
When they tuck us in, the quilt will fold
gently over our eyes. They will tell us
the tale of hanging iron curtains to divide
a city. They will speak of the spider sent
into space, Anita, the webs she spun finer
than any on Earth. In the dark of antiquity
we will map our skull-scapes, each bump
foretelling temperament and shoe size.
We will daub perfume behind our ears
knowing it was once ambergris, which
was once a fetid, fatty white lump, which

was once the pearl of a whale's intestine,
which was once the irritant squid beak
lingering after the meal was long over,
greased until it slid free of the body.
We will corset our chests in whalebone,
knowing every heart has its Jonah song.

PROPOSAL

Show me a tent of well-dressed witnesses
and I'll show you how a circus catches fire:

elephants trying to squeeze down the aisle,
monkeys dancing from pole to hot pole

until the roof collapses. Will you be water?
Will you be ashes? Will you be enough gauze

for a gown? In the stampede, a woman runs
ten yards before noticing the hand she holds

is not her husband's. She keeps running.
Do you blame her? Convince me eternity

is just this art of surviving, over and over.
Promise you're worth my weight in burning.